hide
this
italian
book

APA Publications
New York London

D1382860

hide
this
italian
book

Contacting the Editors
Every effort has been made to provide accurate information in this publication, but changes are inevitable. The publisher cannot be responsible for any resulting loss, inconvenience or injury. We would appreciate it if readers would call our attention to any errors or outdated information. We also welcome your suggestions; if you come across a relevant expression not in our phrase book, please contact us:
Hide This, APA Publications, 58 Borough High Street,
London SE1 1XF, United Kingdom.
Email: language@apaguide.co.uk

First Printing: 2007
2nd edition, March 2013
Printed in China by CTPS

Writer: Eve-Alice Roustang-Stoller
Head of Language: Kate Drynan
Design: Beverley Speight
Illustrator: Kyle Webster

inside

the initiation

Admittance to Italian culture requires more than just knowing a handful of expressions. If you really wanna get in, you've gotta know slang, street speak, and swear words. Hide This Italian Book has what it takes so you can talk the talk. No grammar lessons, verb conjugations, or any rules here—just the language that's actually spoken in Italy today—from the most intimate encounters (and, yeah, we're talking sex) to technology know-how (email, IM, text messaging, Facebook, Twitter).

Stuff you gotta know

It's assumed you already know a little bit of the Italian language. Most of the expressions provided can be applied to both guys and girls. You'll see if the word or phrase can be applied to ♂**guys** alone and when it's for ♀**girls** only.

In case you're uncertain about how to pronounce something in the book and don't want to sound like a fool, go online: **www.insightguides.com/hidethis** and listen up. You may want to lower the volume…

Watch out for…

We've labeled the hottest language with **Hot Spots**, so you can easily gauge just how "bad" the expression really is. You'll see:

 These are pretty crude and crass —use with caution (or not).

 Ouch! Be very careful! Totally offensive, completely inappropriate, and downright nasty terms are labeled with this symbol.

We're dealing with real-life Italian in this book and, therefore, we tell you what the closest English equivalent is—so you know when to use each word, phrase, or expression.

TOP TIPS on what's incredibly HOT and what's not!

 X-RATED Streetwise SLANG that's really vulgar or SHOCKING.

 Essential COOL FACTS that may seem too cool to be true.

 "I can't believe I said that" and more.. EMBARRASSING STORIES

Finally

You know that language is constantly changing—what's in today may be out tomorrow. So, if you come across anything in this book that's no longer said, or learn a cool expression that hasn't been included, let us know; we'd love to hear from you. Send us an email at language@apaguide.com

This book isn't labeled "Un-Censored" for nothing! This isn't the language you wanna use around your boss, relatives, or your new boy- or girlfriend's parents…got it? The stuff that's in here is pretty hot. If you wanna say it in public, that's up to you. But we are not taking the rap (like responsibility and liability) for any mistakes you make—these include, but are not limited to, verbal abuse, fist fights, smackdowns, and/or arrests that may ensue from your usage of the words and expressions in **Hide This Italian Book.**

- say hello and goodbye
- ask what's up?

1. BASIC
EXPRESSIONS

Ciao! Come va?
Hi, how are you?
Simple, but popular.

A bello! A bella!
Hey beautiful!
You'll hear this a lot a lot in southern Italy. If you want to sound like a local, shout it.

Ma guarda chi si vede!
Look who's here! (Literally: Look who is to be seen!)
Say it when you bump into someone you haven't seen in a long time. This includes long-lost "boyfriends" or "girlfriends".

Ma guarda chi c'è!
Look who's here!
Say it with enthusiasm and show your surprise.

BACI, BACI!
In Italy, people traditionally greet each other by shaking hands and with a kiss (bacio - baci in the plural) on each cheek. Nowadays, this is done only with relatives and the elderly. Want to be fashionable? Drop the handshake and just kiss on each cheek. Afraid to get too close? A handshake is a safe, though standard, alternative.

HOW YOU DOIN'?!

– **Come andiamo?** How's it going?
– **Bene grazie.** Good, thanks.

– **Tutto bene?** Is everything fine?
– **Tutto a posto.** Everything's OK.
"Tutto bene" is an elegant way to ask how someone is.
*Alternatively, **"tutto a posto"** is less formal.*

– **Hey! Come ti va la vita?** *Hey! How's life?*
– **Sto da favola!** Wonderful! *(Literally: I'm in a fairy tale!)*

– **Hey, come butta?** Hey, how're things?
– **Butta bene / male.** Things are looking good / bad.

– **Allora…? Che si dice?** So…? What's up?
or
– **Che mi racconti?** What's going on?
– **Sto di merda.** I feel like shit.

– **Allora… novità?** So…what's new?
– **Guarda, sto da panico.** Well, I'm totally stressed.
or
– **Guarda, sto da Dio.** Well, I feel divine.

– **Come stai?** How are you?
– **Sto… / Si tira avanti…** I'm getting by…

– **Come va la vita?** How's life?
– **Così così. / 'nsomma.** So-so.

quick exits

Ci sentiamo!
Let's stay in touch! *(Literally: We'll hear from each other!)*

Fatti sentire / vedere, mi raccomando!
Call me! / Come see me!
Say this to someone you'd like to see again.

Allora… ci si vede!
So…see you!
Say this when you've already made plans to meet up later.

Alla prossima.
See you again.
The classy way to say bye to a friend you'd like to see again.

Vado verso casa… A dopo!
Goin' home… See you later!
Reserve this expression for your closest friends.

Allora… stammi bene.
So…take care.
Say it to someone who needs TLC.

Vado… Ci si becca in giro.
I'm goin'… We'll see each other around.
This one is sarcastic—you won't be seeing them.

ALLORA
By now you will have seen the word "allora" used quite a bit. "Allora…", "So…", or "Well…", is the perfect filler. Use it when you're gathering your thoughts, when you need a pause, or when you want to sound like a local. It's also the perfect start to a question and an ideal way to change the topic of conversation.

- from chatting up to finishing a relationship
- flatter and flirt with ease
- reject a loser

2. HOOKING UP, BREAKING UP

pick-up lines

Vuoi bere qualcosa?
Would you like a drink?
The tried and tested line that seems to work.

Scusa... hai da accendere?
Excuse me,...do you have a light?
The best way to spark a conversation without committing yourself.

Ma... non ci siamo già visti prima?
But...haven't we met before?
Arch an eyebrow, tilt your head—this one may be believable.

Vuoi ballare?
Do you want to dance?
You've got the moves, right?!

CHEESY PICK-UP LINES
These pick-up lines are cheesy, but also great for some laughs. And who knows? They may even work for you!

Scusa... posso dirti che hai degli occhi bellissimi?
Excuse me,...can I tell you that you've got beautiful eyes?
It's not just your eyes that he likes.

Q: Anna? Anna?
A: Non sono Anna... I'm not Anna...
Just calling out a random girl's name may actually get you digits!

Hai da fare per i prossimi 100 anni?
Doing anything for the next 100 years?
He's ready for marriage—are you?

START A CONVERSATION:

– Scusa... Non ci siamo già visti prima?
Excuse me... Haven't we met before?
– Dipende... Che giri hai?
It depends... Where do you hang out?
(Literally: What are your circles?)
or
– Scusa ma sto aspettando qualcuno!
Sorry, but I'm expecting someone.

you flirt!

IS HE OR SHE HOT?

Quella tipa è...	That girl is...
una gran figa*	
una gran gnocca*	really sexy.
bona da paura.	good (in bed).
uno schianto.	a knockout.

Quel tipo è...	That guy is...
un sano della Madonna.**	really good-looking.
un figo da paura.	a hot, cool guy.
un gran manzo.	a great guy.
	(Literally: a great bull)

**Guys may talk about a girl being a "figa", literally, fig, or "gnocca", literally, a potato dumpling, among themselves, but would never say it to a girl's face; it can be derogatory.*

***Use "della Madonna" (literally: of the Madonna) to describe something or someone—and bring it, him, or her to a higher level...*

DOUBLE MEANINGS..

Food + sex = "**figa**". Some speculate that "**figa**", a northern Italian variant of "**fico**", fig, became a slang word for vulva because of the similarities in shape between the two. Don't use the term liberally: it's vulgar in some regions of Italy. Try not to confuse "**figa**" with "**fico**" or "**figo**" —both of which mean cool!

tell them they're hot:

FOR HER:

Franca, sei...	Franca, you're…
speciale.	special.
dolce.	sweet.
bellissima.	incredibly beautiful.

FOR HIM:

Mauro,...	Mauro,…
sei speciale.	you're special.
sei troppo forte.	you're really amazing.
	(Literally: you're too strong)
non sei come gli altri.	you're not like the other guys.

flat-out refusals

No, guarda, stasera non è proprio serata.
I'm not in the right mood tonight.
A subtle way to say no thanks.

Scusa, ma sto aspettando qualcun altro.
Sorry, but I'm expecting someone.
It doesn't have to be true.

Evapora!
Disappear! *(Literally: Evaporate!)*
Clear and to the point!

Lasciami in pace!
Leave me alone!
Brutal, but sometimes it's the only way to get rid of somebody.

Ho di meglio da fare.
I have something better to do.
Snobbish, but it'll work.

Guarda… puoi andare!
Look…you're excused!
He's not good enough to even be in your presence.

Fa / Fai dei metri!
Take a hike! *(Literally: Do some meters!)*
He probably needs the exercise.

PREPARE FOR THE WORST

– Sai che sei proprio figa?
You know, you're really hot?

– Senti… Fai dei metri! Listen up… Take a hike!

breaking up

**FALLEN OUT OF LOVE? HERE ARE SOME OF THE BEST WAYS TO
BREAK IT OFF...**

Ho bisogno di tempo per riflettere.
I need time to think about it.
In fact, it's the beginning of the end.

È finita.
It's over between us.
That's right!

È meglio farla finita.
It's better to break up.
It's a gentle way to let someone down.

Rimaniamo amici.
Let's just be friends.
Say it if you mean it!

Con te ho chiuso!
I'm over you! (Literally: I closed with you!)
Give him or her some closure.

spreading the word

SO IT'S ALL OVER? LET YOUR FRIENDS DO THE TALKING.

Lei...	She...
ha chiuso con lui.	ended it.
lo ha mandato a quel paese.	sent him packing.
lo ha mandato affanculo.	told him to stick it up his ass.

RATED X

NASTY THINGS TO CALL YOUR EX

È uno/a…	He/She is a…
sfigato/a.	loser.
cesso.	scumbag. *(Literally: a toilet)*
mostro.	monster.
Guarda che…	Look, what a…
schifo d'uomo.	repulsive man.
puttaniere. ♂ **HOT!**	slut. *(Literally: a man who sleeps with prostitutes)*
cozza.	dog. *(Literally: mussel)*
scorfano. ♀ **HOT!**	dog. *(Literally: scorpion fish)*
chiavica.	dog. *(Literally: drain, sewer)*
puttanella.	little whore.

- get romantic—from kissing to sex
- the best ways to say we did it
- safe sex and STDs

3. LOVE
and SEX

ABBIAMO UNA TRESCA.

MI PIACI DA MORIRE.

in the mood for love?

FIRST COMES THE ATTRACTION...

Abbiamo una tresca.

We're having an affair.

Ci facciamo delle storie.   NORTHERN ITALY

We're just seeing each other.

(Literally: We have some stories.)

THEN ROMANCE...

Ci stiamo frequentando. / Stiamo uscendo.

We're going out.

È il mio ragazzo. / È la mia ragazza.

He's my boyfriend. / She's my girlfriend.

FINALLY, SEX!

Siamo stati a letto insieme.

We went to bed.

(Literally: We were in bed together.)

hot n' heavy

HOW TO GET THINGS GOING...

Ho una gran voglia di baciarti.
I'm dying to kiss you.

Un bacino, per favore...
A little kiss, please...

Mi piaci da morire.
I adore you.

Ho voglia di te.
I want you.

Voglio fare l'amore con te.
I want to make love to you.

sweet talk

NEED A PET NAME FOR YOUR LOVER? TRY ONE OF THESE.

Mi dai un bacio,...	Give me a kiss,...
tesoro.	my treasure.
topolina.	my dear. *(Literally: little mouse)*
luce dei miei occhi.	my sunshine.
	(Literally: light of my eyes)
passerotto.	my little bird. *(Literally: sparrow)*
bimba.	baby.
cucciolo/a.	my darling. *(Literally: puppy)*
dolcezza.	honey. *(Literally: sweetness)*
piccola.	my little one.
stella.	my love. *(Literally: star)*
patatina.	my sweetie. *(Literally: small potato)*
ciccio/a.	my dear. *(Literally: fat)*

safe sex

BE CAREFUL! YOU'LL PROBABLY NEED THESE:

Hai un...?
preservativo
guanto (Literally: glove)
goldone
cappuccio (Literally: hood)

Do you have a condom?

Prendi la pillola?
Are you on the pill?

Hai il diaframma?
Did you put the diaphragm in?

Hai la spirale?
Do you use an IUD?

STDs 101

ASK THE RIGHT QUESTIONS BEFORE THINGS GET TOO HOT.

– **Hai fatto il test per l'aids?** Have you had an AIDS test?
– **Certo, tutto a posto!** Sure! Everything's OK!

AND BE PREPARED FOR THE RESPONSE...

Quel ragazzo ha...	He has...
Quella ragazza ha...	She has...
una malattia venerea.	a venereal disease.
la sifilide.	syphillis.
l'aids.	AIDS.
l'herpes.	herpes.
l'epatite c.	hepatitis C.

COUNTLESS WAYS TO SAY WE DID IT!

Abbiamo passato la notte assieme.
We spent the night together.

Abbiamo fatto sesso.
We had sex.

È successo quello che doveva succedere.
And what was meant to happen, happened.

Abbiamo trombato come ricci.
We fucked like rabbits.
(Literally: We fucked like hedgehogs.)

Finalmente me l'ha data!
Finally she surrendered!
(Literally: She finally gave me her vagina!)

THERE ARE SO MANY DIFFERENT WAYS TO SAY "MAKING LOVE", AND SOME OF THEM CAN BE DOWNRIGHT DIRTY. GUYS: DON'T SAY ANY OF THE BELOW TO YOUR GIRL. THESE EXPRESSIONS ARE RESTRICTED TO THE LOCKER ROOM!

Mi piace un casino...   I love...
scopare.   fucking. (Literally: sweeping [with a broom])

trombare.   having casual sex. (Literally: playing the trumpet)

chiavare.   screwing.
fottere / ciulare.   fucking. (Literally: swiping)

the verdict

Lei è...   She is…

una brava ragazza.   a good girl.

una ragazza a posto.   a respectable girl.

una suora.   a nun.

una santarellina.   a false saint.

una ragazza di facili costumi.   a slut. (Literally: a girl of easy virtue)

HOT! **una bomba da sesso.**   a sex bomb.

Lui è...   He's…

un cavaliere.

un gentleman.   a gentleman.

un bravo ragazzo.   a good guy.

un ragazzo per bene.   a respectable guy.

un farfallone.   a Casanova.

un bastardo.   a bastard.

un gigolò.   a gigolo.

HOT! **un animale da letto.**   a sex animal. (Literally: an animal for bed)

EXTRA HOT! **una macchina da sesso.**   a sex machine.

HOT! **uno sciupafemmine.**   a male slut.

This popular word is a combination of "sciupare", to spoil or ruin, and "femmine", meaning female.

4. GAY and LESBIAN LIFE

GLI PIACCIONO GLI UOMINI.

LE PIACCIONO LE DONNE.

is he gay?

WHETHER YOU'RE GAY OR HAVE A FRIEND WHO IS, HERE'S THE LANGUAGE YOU NEED TO TALK ABOUT HOMOSEXUALITY.

Franco è...	Franco is...
omosessuale.	homosexual.
gay.	gay.
diverso.	"different".

Paolo è...
frocio.
This was once an offensive term, but is now used by the gay community.

finocchio.   (Literally: fennel)
An old-fashioned term usually said by older folks, but it's still used.

ricchione.   (Literally: big ear)
Also spelled "recchione"; it comes from Naples, but is known everywhere.

Paolo is gay.

un culattone.
The word, mainly used in northern Italy, comes from "culo", ass.

un busone.   veneto, emilia
(Literally: big ass[hole])
un checca.

Francesca è lesbica.
Francesca is a lesbian.
Warning! If used in the wrong context, all of these terms can be derogatory.

TABOO

Italy is mainly a Catholic country and, therefore, homosexuality is, for the most part, still taboo. The more liberal Italian towns are often tolerant of gay lifestyles. Bologna is considered the "gay capital" of Italy. Many gay-friendly locations can also be found throughout Rome and its suburbs. Milan is another city in which gay bars and clubs thrive. For gay guys and lesbians who want to relax, try Versilia, an area in Tuscany which is gay-friendly; the same can be said about the coast of Romagna.

is he gay?

È bisex.
He/She is bi.
Le piace provare di tutto.
He/She likes to try everything.
Le piace andare sia con gli uomini che con le donne.
She likes to go both ways. (Literally: She likes to go with both men and women.)
Maurizio è un vero metrosessuale.
Maurizio is a real metrosexual.

METROSEXUALS

The typical Italian metrosexual is male, a very snappy dresser, knows about everything designer (especially Italian), and most importantly — he is heterosexual! This may seem unbelievable girls, but it's true. This guy may in fact be everything you've ever wanted in a boyfriend, with one very important fringe benefit: he'll happily go shopping with you. Be warned though — things may get messy when you find out his wardrobe is far superior to yours…

coming out

Andrea è dell'altra sponda.
Andrea is from the other side.
(Literally: Andrea is from the other riverbank.)

Gli piacciono gli uomini.
He likes men.

Fabio è andato via con il suo nuovo amichetto.
Fabio left with his new gay partner.
(Literally: Fabio left with his little friend.)

Luca è troppo effemminato.
Luca is so effeminate.

Le piacciono le donne.
She likes women.

È una maschiaccia.
She's a tomboy.

È sicuramente una lesbo.
She is definitely a lesbo.

party time

FIND THAT FUN HANGOUT.

Conosci...	Do you know...
una discoteca gay?	a gay dance club?
una discoteca lesbo?	a lesbian dance club?
un pub gay?	a gay bar?

- cheer for your team
- talk about soccer
- in the gym
- gambling and gaming

5. SPORT
and GAMES

cheers

MOTIVATE THE PLAYERS WITH THESE.

Forza Juve!

Go for it Juve!

"Juve" is one of Italy's national soccer teams.

Forza Milan alè alè!

Go for it Milan! Cheer up!

Vai così!

Go this way!

Tira!

Throw (the ball)!

Passala!

Pass (the ball)!

Siamo solo noi.

We are the champions.

This refers to a famous song by Vasco Rossi.

È uno spettacolo.

What a performance. (Literally: It's a spectacle.)

Facci sognare!

Make us dream!

FACT

SONGS

In Italy, people will literally scream anything to motivate their team—and they will often personalize songs about their favorite team or players. A very popular song in Rome is "Ma che siete venuti a fa'?" What did you come for? What they really mean is: You came to lose!

compliments

USE THESE EXPRESSIONS TO CELEBRATE YOUR TEAM'S SPECTACULAR MOVES AND SHOTS.

Che partita!
What a move!

È stata una partita...!	It was a/an...move!
favolosa	fabulous
fantastica	fantastic
mitica	amazing
	(Literally: mythical)
indimenticabile	unforgettable
unica	unique
da paura	terrific
È stato un goal...	It was a/an...goal.
della Madonna.	wonderful (Literally: from the Madonna)
divino.	heavenly
	(Literally: divine)
spettacolare.	spectacular
Ha giocato...	He played...
da Dio.	like a god.
divinamente.	divinely.
da fuoriclasse.	like a champion.

Un attacco formidabile!
An amazing attack!
Se la sono sudata.
They had to sweat to win.
Ce la siamo meritata!
We earned it!

È stato/a...!	It was...!
un partitone	a great game
una gran partita	
una partita storica	an historic game
la partita del secolo	the game of the century

insults

HARASSING THE REFEREE AND HUMILIATING THE OPPONENT IS PART OF YOUR JOB AS A SPECTATOR.

Arbitro cornuto!
Referee, you're a sucker!

Arbitro venduto!
Referee, you sold yourself!

Che arbitro del cazzo!
What a shit referee!

Arbitro bastardo!
Referee, you're a bastard!

Ma che cazzo fai, coglione?!
What the hell are you doing, dick?!

RATED

LOVE SOCCER, "CALCIO"? A SOCCER GAME IS THE PERFECT SCENARIO TO USE ALL THE DIRTY WORDS YOU KNOW. HERE IS A GOOD SELECTION; WE SUGGEST YOU USE THEM INSIDE THE STADIUM ONLY.

Figlio di puttana!	Son of a bitch!
Stronzo!	Turd!
Pezzo di merda!	Piece of shit!
Vaffanculo!	Fuck off!

X RATED

MAY WE SUGGEST YOU USE THESE ONES INSIDE THE STADIUM ONLY!

Tira quella cazzo di palla!
Throw that fucking ball!

Sei un coglione!
You dick! (Literally: You're a testicle!)

Cazzo, tirala in porta!
Shit, kick at the goal!

Corri in difesa!
Get on defense!

Marcalo stretto!
Play tight defense! (Literally: Score tight!)

Che cappella!
What a fuck-up!

but, there's more to life than soccer!

Ti piace…?	Do you like…?
il baseball	baseball
il basket	basketball
la box	boxing
la formula 1	Formula 1
il ciclismo	cycling
il rugby	rugby
il monopattino	skateboarding

il pattinaggio inline	inline skating
l'atletica leggera	track and field
la pallavolo	volleyball
il sollevamento pesi	weightlifting
le arti marziali	martial arts
il surf	surfing
il windsurf	windsurfing
il kite-surf	kitesurfing
il nuoto	swimming
la pallanuoto	water polo
lo sci nautico	water skiing
lo sci	skiing
lo snowboard	snowboarding

in the gym

Vado…	I go…
in palestra.	to the gym.
a fare un po' di movimento.	exercising.
	(Literally: move myself a bit)
ad aerobica.	to do aerobics.
a far pesi.	to lift weights.
a fare body building.	body building.
a fare gag.	to do the BLT workout.
BLT =	butt, legs, tummy
a fare spinning.	spinning.
a fare un po' di cyclette.	to use the fitness bike.
a fare un po' di tapis roulant.	to use the treadmill.
a fare acqua gym.	to do water aerobics.
Dai che ce la fai!	
Come on! You can do it!	

Ancora uno sforzo!
One more try!

Non ce la faccio più!

I'm exhausted!

Sono...	**I'm...**
esausto/a.	**exhausted.**
sfinito/a.	**run-down.**
stanco/a.	**tired.**
morto/a.	**dead.**
arrivato/a.	**done. (Literally: arrived)**
cotto/a.	**fried. (Literally: cooked)**

Sto sudando come un cammello!
The sweat is pouring out of me!
(Literally: I'm sweating like a camel!)

cooling down

Avete...?	Do you have...?
la sauna	a sauna
il bagno turco	a steam room
la doccia	a shower
i massaggi	massage service

Non dimenticare...	Don't forget...
i pantaloncini.	the shorts.
la maglietta.	the T-shirt.
l'asciugamano.	the towel.
la tuta.	the leotard and leggings.

gambling

PRACTICE THESE EXPRESSIONS BEFORE YOU PUT YOUR MONEY DOWN AND RISK IT ALL.

Hai già puntato?
Did you place your bet?

Su chi hai puntato?
What did you bet on?

Ho puntato 100€ sul rosso.
I bet €100 on red.

Ho fatto 13!
I got 13!

Ho vinto la lotteria!
I won the lottery!

Ho avuto un culo della Madonna!
I was really lucky! (Literally: I had a great ass!)

Mi hanno fottuto!
They screwed me!

Sono rovinato/a.
I'm ruined.

Ho la sfiga che mi perseguita.
Luck is against me.

TIP

THE NATIONAL SOCCER LOTTERY GAME

Italians have combined the best of two worlds: sports and gambling. "Totocalcio" is a national soccer lottery game; simply fill in the coupon with the teams you think will win. If you manage to get the goal of 14 points, you're awarded a cash prize. A smaller prize is also awarded to those who get 13 points. Another popular game is the virtual "Fantacalcio". You create your own team with current players and organize your own championships. The results are based on how your players perform during the real matches!

video games
VIDEO GAME LINGO AT ITS BEST.

Facciamo una partita alla play?
Want to play with the PlayStation®?

Facciamo un doppio?
Shall we play together?

Colpiscilo!
Get him!

Sparagli!
Shoot at him!

Fallo fuori!
Kill him!

L'ho steso!
I hit him!

L'ho ammazzato!
I killed him!

L'ho abbattuto!
I knocked him down!

BOARD AND CARD GAMES
Though home video games are popular, board and card games are also still a popular choice. Many Italians love to socialize and would rather play group games than stay at home with their video games.

6.SHOPPING

shop talk

Dov'è il reparto…?	Where is the…department?
donne / uomini	women's / men's
articoli sportivi	sportswear
costumi da bagno	swimwear
calzature	shoe
profumeria	cosmetics
Cercavo qualcosa di…	I'm looking for something…
sobrio.	simple. (Literally: sober)
elegante.	elegant.
sportivo.	sporty.
carino.	cute.
sfizioso.	special.
provocante.	provocative, sexy.
originale.	original, unique.

FACT

ITALY IS A SHOPPER'S PARADISE…

Visit Milan for high fashion or Florence for top-quality merchandise. Love shoes? Visit the beautiful Marche, a region known all over the world for their quality leather shoes. Are cars your passion? Take a tour of the famous Ferrari Museum in Maranello. Want the best souvenirs? Drop in on Venice and pick up some authentic masks and other Venetian handicrafts. Don't forget that Viareggio also has an historic Carnival; you can find top quality souvenirs there as well. Looking for the best deal? Just about every major Italian brand has a factory outlet store, "spaccio aziendale". You'll get deep discounts on everything, from designer hats to famous footwear.

MARKETS

In Italy, shops aren't the only places where you can buy clothes and other merchandise. There are tons of unique markets all over the country. In Rome there is the famous "Porta Portese". Here, you can find just about everything: from food and drink to clothes and accessories. You can also find the latest designs by Italy's top designers. But beware: many of the designer items you'll find at these markets are knock-offs!

need some help?

HERE ARE SOME TYPICAL SENTENCES EVERY SALES CLERK WILL USE TO TEMPT YOU.

Posso aiutarti?
Can I help you?

Posso esserti utile?
Can I help you? (Literally: Can I be of help?)

Cercavi qualcosa in particolare?
Are you looking for something in particular?

Vuoi vedere qualcos'altro?
Do you want to see anything else?

Se hai bisogno chiedi pure!
If you need something, please ask me!

asking for assistance

Hai anche taglie più grandi?
Do you have bigger sizes?

Hai la 42?
Do you have size 42?

Hai anche altri colori?
Do you have it in other colors?

No, non è il mio genere / stile.
No, it's not my style.

Cercavo qualcosa di più giovanile.
I was looking for something more youthful.

Posso provare questo paio di pantaloni?
Could I try on these pants?

Dov'è lo spogliatoio?
Where is the fitting room?

Dove avete…?	Where can I find…?
i CD	CDs
i DVD	DVDs
le cartoline	postcards
i libri	books
giornali e riviste	newspapers and magazines

CONFRONTED BY AN ANNOYING SALES CLERK?
– **Ciao! Posso aiutarti?** Hi! Can I help you?
– **No, davo solo un'occhiata in giro.**
   No, I'm just looking around.

how much?

Quanto costa?
How much is it?

Quanto viene?
How much is it? (Literally: How much does it come?)
A familiar way to ask.

Posso pagare con il bancomat?
Can I pay with a bank / debit card?

Posso pagare con la carta di credito?
Can I pay with a credit card?

Accettate assegni?
Do you accept checks?

money, money, money

Mi presti…?

un po' di soldi

un po' di quattrini *(Literally: some pennies)*

due verdoni *(Literally: two big bills)*

Can you lend me
some money?

what a steal

Facciamo 10€ e non se ne parla più?
Let's make it €10 and drop it?
(Literally: Should we make it €10 and not speak of it any more?)

Mi vuoi rovinare?
Do you want to ruin me?

È stato un affare!
It was a bargain!

Quel negozio ha dei prezzi niente male.
That shop's prices aren't bad.

Quel negozio ha della bella roba.
That shop has good stuff.

Mi è costato un occhio della testa!
It cost me an arm and a leg!
(Literally: It cost me an eye from my head!)

È un furto!
It's a total rip-off!

Mi è costato lo stipendio!
It cost my entire salary!

Mi hanno salassato.
They robbed me. (Literally: They fleeced me.)

In quel negozio sono cari ammazzati!
That shop is deathly expensive!

7. FASHION

fashion talk

Questi pantaloni...	These pants...
sono fighi.	are cool.
sono un tot fighi. NORTHERN ITALY	are really cool.
sono una figata.	are cool.
sono troppo belli.	are so nice. (Literally: too nice)
sono all'ultimo grido.	are stylish. (Literally: in the latest shout)
sono alla moda.	are in fashion.
sono in / out.	are in / out.
sono passati di moda.	are out of fashion.
sono da zia.	are old-fashioned. (Literally: in the style of my aunt)
fanno schifo.	are gross.
Quella gonna...	That skirt...
ti sta da Dio!	looks divine on you!
sembra fatta apposta per te.	was made for you.
sembra fatta su misura per te.	looks custom-made for you.
ti sta troppo bene.	totally suits you.
t'ingrassa.	makes you look fat.
ti fa più magra.	is slimming.
Francesca...	Francesca...
è troppo alla moda.	is so fashionable.
si veste figa.	always looks cool.
si veste troppo bene.	is always well-dressed.
si veste un po' da fighetta.	always dresses like a preppie.
si veste troppo da sfigata.	always dresses like a loser.

fashion disaster

Alessandro...	Alessandro...
si veste troppo male!	is always dressed so badly!
è completamente fuori moda!	is totally out of fashion!
si veste da barbone.	is dressed like a bum.

wardrobe essentials

un cappellino
a cap

una maglietta
T-shirt

una giacca
a jacket

un jeans
jeans

un paio di slip
briefs

un maglione
a sweater

la borsa
bag

le scarpi
shoes

boxer
boxers

la borsetta
purse

le occhiali da sole
sunglasses

un reggiseno
a bra

la canottiera
top

un bikini
bikini

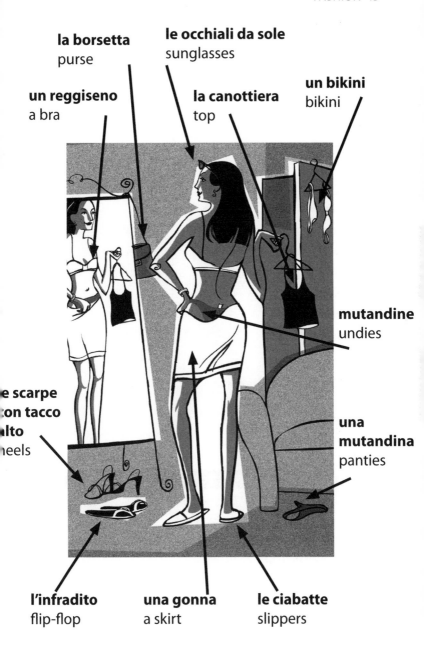

mutandine
undies

**e scarpe
con tacco
alto**
heels

**una
mutandina**
panties

l'infradito
flip-flop

una gonna
a skirt

le ciabatte
slippers

make yourself beautiful

Mi passi…?	Can you give me (some/a/an)…?
il fondotinta	make-up
la terra	face powder
il fard	blush
la cipria	powder
l'eyeliner	eyeliner
la matita per gli occhi	eye pencil
il correttore	concealer
l'ombretto	eye shadow
il rossetto	lipstick
il lucidalabbra	lip gloss
il burro di cacao	lip balm
il mascara	mascara

FACT

BEAUTY PRODUCTS FOR MEN..

Think that only women are into their looks? Think again! Italian men can spend almost as much as women on beauty products and treatments. This includes hair and skin products, hair styling, and even waxing (we won't tell where)! Now you know why those Italian guys look so good…

in the bathroom

♂ FOR HIM..

Dove posso trovare…?	Where can I find…?
un rasoio	a razor
della crema da barba	some shaving cream
del dopobarba	some aftershave
del gel	some hair gel
del profumo	some cologne

♀ FOR HER..

Mi servirebbe…	I need…
un pennello per il fard.	a make-up brush.
una spugnetta per il fondotinta.	a make-up sponge.
una pinzetta.	tweezers.

Hai…?	Do you have…?
una pastiglia per i dolori mestruali	pills for cramps
un assorbente	a pad
un tampone	a tampon
un po' di crema per le mani	some hand cream

pamper yourself

Vorrei…	I'd like…
un massaggio facciale.	a facial.
una ceretta completa.	a complete wax.
una ceretta nella zona bikini.	a bikini wax.
una pulizia del viso.	a face cleansing.
un massaggio anticellulite.	a cellulite massage.
un massaggio rilassante.	a relaxing massage.
farmi le unghie.	a manicure.
un pedicure.	a pedicure.
farmi le sopracciglia.	my eyebrows waxed.
fare una lampada.	a tanning session.

FACT

THE "BEAUTY-FARM".

Italy is famous for the "beauty-farm", a place to go for skincare, treatments, and massage. Some are just day spas while others are hotel spas that cater to longer breaks. Visit one that has a hot water spring and enjoy luxury treatments like massage or mud therapy alongside a dip in the thermal baths. Proponents say that the thermal water can help cure conditions such as respiratory problems, skin conditions, arthritis, and more. Just keep in mind that water temperatures can reach almost 37.7 degrees C—that's 100 degrees F!

crowning glory

Hai un parrucchiere di fiducia da consigliarmi?
Can you recommend a good hair stylist?

Vorrei…	I'd like…
farmi una tinta.	to dye my hair.
farmi un riflesso.	some highlights.
farmi le mèches.	some streaks in my hair.
tagliarmi i capelli.	a haircut.

Me li stiri con la piastra?
Can you flat iron my hair?

Mi fai un taglio scalato?
Can you layer my hair?

Vorrei farmi una messa in piega.
I'd like to have my hair styled.
This orginally meant set in rollers!

Sai dov'è un barbiere?
Do you know where the barber shop is?

Li vorrei rasati.
I'd like to have my head shaved.

Mi piace quel ragazzo…	I like that boy…
con i capelli ricci.	with curly hair.
rasato.	with shaved head.
biondo.	with blonde hair.
moro.	with dark hair.
con i capelli castani.	with brown hair.
con i capelli rossi.	with red hair.

body alterations

È completamente rifatta!
She is totally re-made!
Meaning: She's had a ton of plastic surgery.

Si è rifatta…	She had…
	(Literally: She remade…)
il seno.	a boob job.
il naso.	a nose job.
il doppiomento.	a "double chin" removed.
il fondoschiena.	butt surgery.
	Implants or liposuction.

Si è fatta un lifting al viso.
She had a face lift.

Si è siliconata…	She enhanced her…
le tette.	boobs.
le labbra.	lips.
le chiappe.	butt.

Ha il piercing…	He/She has a/an…
	piercing.
all'ombelico.	belly button
al sopracciglio.	eyebrow
sul capezzolo.	nipple
al naso.	nose
sul mento.	chin
lì.	genital (Literally: there)

È tatuato.
He's got a tattoo.

Ha un tatuaggio troppo figo.
He/She has a cool tattoo.

8. BODY

body beautiful

ALL ABOUT HER...

Anna ha...	Anna has...
un gran fisico.	a great body.
un fisico della Madonna.	an incredible body.
un gran telaio	a great frame.
una bella carrozzeria.	a good structure.
un fisico mozzafiato.	a breathtaking body.
un corpo da far girar la testa.	a body that makes your head spin.
un fisichetto niente male.	a nice body.
due gran tette.	nice boobs.
due bocce favolose.	fabulous boobs. (Literally: fabulous bowls)
un culo bello sodo.	a firm butt.
due gambe da favola.	fabulous legs.

HOT!

ALL ABOUT HIM...

Fabio ha...	Fabio has...
un fondoschiena niente male.	a nice backside.
un gran fisico.	a great body.
dei gran muscoli.	good muscles.
la tartaruga.	a six-pack. (Literally: the tortoise)
un fisico da palestrato.	a sculpted body. "Palestrato" comes from "palestra", gym.
la panza da birra.	a beer belly.
una gran trippa.	a big belly. (Literally: a big tripe)
dei gran rotoli.	big rolls.

butt ugly

Giovanna è fatta a pera.
Giovanna is shaped like a pear.
Not a positive trait…

Anna è praticamente quadrata.
Anna is shapeless.
(Literally: Anna is practically square-shaped).
Ouch!

Serena è una tavola da surf.
Serena is a surfboard.
She's that flat?!

Stefania è una botte.
Stefania is fat. (Literally: Stefania is a barrel.)

Marco è un ciccione.
Marco is a fattie.
"Ciccione" comes from the word "ciccia", which is what children use to say meat.

Luisa è…	Luisa is…
cicciottella / rotondetta.	chubby.
grossa.	fat. (Literally: big)
ben piazzata / robusta.	robust.

A nice way to state the obvious.

body parts

HOT! **WARNING! THE LANGUAGE ON THIS PAGE CAN BE PRETTY HOT!**

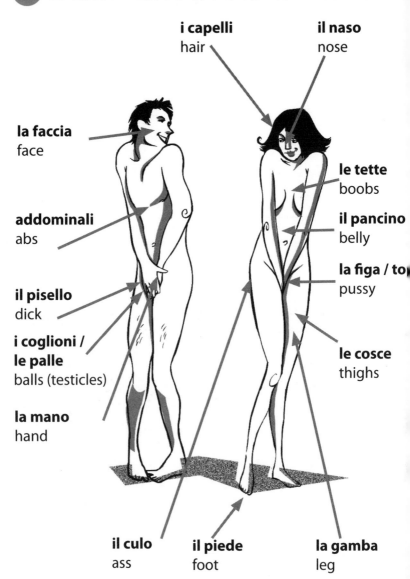

i capelli
hair

il naso
nose

la faccia
face

le tette
boobs

addominali
abs

il pancino
belly

il pisello
dick

la figa / to|
pussy

i coglioni /
le palle
balls (testicles)

le cosce
thighs

la mano
hand

il culo
ass

il piede
foot

la gamba
leg

skin problems

Mi è spuntato un brufolo sul naso!
I got a pimple on my nose!

Sono pieno/a di brufoli!
I'm full of pimples!

Sono pieno/a di punti neri!
I'm full of blackheads!

Mi puzzano le ascelle / i piedi.
My armpits / feet stink.

Ho dei peli che sembro un orso!
I'm as hairy as a bear!

body functions

Vado alla toilette.
I'm going to the toilet.

Vado in bagno.
I'm going to the bathroom.

Vado a fare la pipì / popò.
I'm going to pee / poop.

Vado a fare la cacca.
I'm going to take a crap.

Vado a cagare.
I'm going to take a shit.

Vado in seduta.
I'm going to a session.
Meaning: You'll be in the restroom for some time.

Devo andare di corpo.
I need to poop. (Literally: I need to give from the body.)

gross

TOTALLY NASTY...

Qualcuno ha fatto uno scoreggione!
Someone farted!

Chi ha fatto una puzzetta?
Who farted? (Literally: Who made a small stink?)

Ha fatto un rutto!
He/She burped!

Che schifo! Hai una caccola nel naso!
That's gross! You have a snot in your nose!

Bleah! Hai i brustolini negli occhi.
Ew! You have goo in your eyes.

Hai qualcosa in mezzo ai denti.
You have something in your teeth.

Hai un brufolone pieno di pus proprio sul naso.
You have a big pimple full of pus on your nose.

Dai, non schiacciarti i brufoli!
Don't squeeze those pimples!

Ha un alito che ti stende!
He/She has toxic breath!

Ha l'alito pesante!
He/She has bad breath! (Literally: He/She has heavy breath!)

HELP OUT A FRIEND IN NEED

– **Hai qualcosa in mezzo ai denti!**
  You have something in your teeth!
– **Davvero? Che imbarazzo!** Really? That's so embarassing!
– **Tieni... uno stuzzicadente.** Here's a toothpick.

help, I'm sick!

Ahiaiai, ho…	Ugh! I have…
la diarrea.	diarrhea.
la caghetta.	the runs. *"Caghetta" is the diminutive of "cacca", poop.*
il mal di mare.	motion sickness.
il mal d'aria.	air sickness.
il mal di stomaco.	stomach pains.
dei crampi terribili.	terrible cramps.
la febbre.	a fever.
l'influenza.	the flu.
il raffreddore.	a cold.
la tosse.	a cough.

Sto di merda.
I feel like shit.

Sto uno schifo.
I feel gross.

Ho un mal di testa atroce.
I have an atrocious headache.

Sto morendo dal dolore.
The pain is killing me.

Non hai una gran bella cera oggi.
You don't look well today.

- phone friends
- communicate online
- talk on the phone
- use text speak

9.MEDIA

call me

Chiamami!
Call me!

Fatti sentire!
Let me hear from you!

Fammi uno squillo più tardi!
Call me later! (Literally: Give me a ring later!)

phone talk

Dove ho messo il mio cellulare / telefonino?
Where did I put my cell phone?
"Telefonino" literally means little phone.

Pronto?
Hello? (Literally: Ready?)

Sì?
Yes?

Chi parla?
Who's speaking?

Mi passi Alessandro per favore?
May I speak with Alessandro please? (Literally: Can you give me Alessandro please?)

C'è Rosa?
Is Rosa there?

Posso parlare con Anna?
Can I speak with Anna?

Sono io!
It's me!

Aspetta un attimo che te la passo.
Hold on a moment, she's coming. (Literally: Wait a moment, I'll give her to you.)

Un attimo solo.
Just a moment.

Non è in casa, la trovi più tardi.
She's not in, you can catch her later.

hang up

Scusa ma devo andare.
Excuse me, but I have to go.

Devo scappare!
I must be off!

Scusa, c'è mia madre che mi sta chiamando!
Excuse me, my mother is calling me!

When all else fails, use this tactic to get off the phone!
Ci sentiamo più tardi?
Can we speak later?
(Literally: Can we hear from each other later?)

Me lo mandi un bacio prima di riattaccare?
Will you send me a kiss before you hang up?

answering machines

Ciao, lasciate un messaggio dopo il bip!
Hi! Leave a message after the beep!

Ciao, sono Luca, mi richiami?
Hi, this is Luca; call me back?

TIP

TEXT SPEAK
Text speak changes all the time but the abbreviations opposite are some old favorites. If at first you don't know how to use it, don't worry, you'll soon pick it up – once you figure out what your friends are trying to say that is.

text talk

Dove 6? [Dove sei?]
Where are you?
"Sei" the number six is spelled the same as "sei", you are.

Ki 6? [Chi sei?]
Who are you?

C sent + tardi! [Ci sentiamo pi tardi!]
Let's talk later.

C ved dopo! [Ci vediamo dopo!]
CUL8TR [See you later.]

M. bene [Molto bene]
very well

Abb. bene [Abbastanza bene]
pretty good

Tr. tardi [Troppo tardi]
too late

Nn so [Non so]
I don't know.

Xk nn 6 venuto? [Perch non sei venuto?]
Why didn't you come?

TVTB [Ti Voglio Tanto Bene]
I love you very much.
Used by friends and lovers.

TAT [Ti Amo Tanto]
I love you so much.

online

Dov'è un Internet caffè?
Where's an internet cafe?

C'è il wireless?
Does it have wireless internet?

Qual è la password Wi-Fi?
What is the WiFi password?

Il WiFi è gratis?
Is the WiFi free?

Avete il Bluetooth
Do you have bluetooth?

Come si accende/spegne il computer?
How do I turn the computer on/off?

Accendi il computer.
Turn on the computer.

Posso…?	Can I…?
collegarmi (a Internet)	access the internet
controllare le e-mail	check email
stampare	print
collegare/ricaricare il	plug in/charge my laptop/
mio portatile/iPhone/iPad?	iPhone/iPad/BlackBerry?
usare Skype?	access Skype?

Quanto costa per un'ora/mezz'ora?
How much per hour/half hour?

Come…?	How do I…?
ci si collega/scollega	connect/disconnect
si fa il login/logout	log on/log off
digiti questo simbolo	type this symbol

Avete uno scanner?
Do you have a scanner?

Posso scaricare della roba?
Can I download some stuff?

Sono in rete / online.
I'm online.

Zippa / Comprimi quel file.
Compress that file.

Apri / Chiudi il documento.
Open / Close the document.

Cancellalo.
Delete it.

L'hai salvato?
Did you save it?

Clicca qui!
Click here!

Non guardare la mia password!
Don't look at my password!

help desk

Il computer…	The computer…
si è bloccato.	froze. (Literally: is blocked)
non dà segni di vita.	doesn't show any signs of life.
non risponde.	doesn't answer.
si è impallato.	is frozen.
è morto.	died.

Il file è…	The file is…
andato perso.	lost.
stato danneggiato.	damaged.
stato eliminato.	deleted.
fottuto.	fucked.

LOOKING FOR SOME COMPUTER HELP?

– **Non riesco ad aprire la mia posta.**
  I can't open my mail.
– **Vuoi che ti aiuti?** Do you want me to help you?
– **Grazie!** Thank you!

email

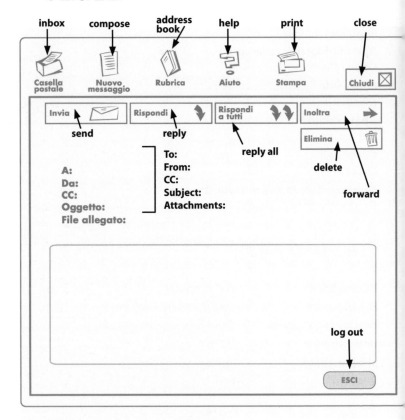

inbox — Casella postale
compose — Nuovo messaggio
address book — Rubrica
help — Aiuto
print — Stampa
close — Chiudi

send — Invia
reply — Rispondi
reply all — Rispondi a tutti
forward — Inoltra
delete — Elimina

A: — To:
Da: — From:
CC: — CC:
Oggetto: — Subject:
File allegato: — Attachments:

log out — ESCI

social media

Ho trovato un sito che è una figata!
I found a cool site!

È il mio sito preferito.
It's my favorite site.

Puoi mandarmi il link?
Can you send me the link?

Sei su Facebook/Twitter?
Are you on Facebook/Twitter?

Qual è il tuo nome utente?
What's your username?

Ti aggiungerò come amico.
I'll add you as a friend.

Ti seguirò su Twitter.
I'll follow you on Twitter.

Seguite...?
Are you following...?

Metterò le foto su Facebook/Twitter.
I'll put the pictures on Facebook/Twitter.

Ti taggherò nelle foto.
I'll tag you in the pictures.

Hai un indirizzo email?
Do you have an email address?

Mi dai la tua mail?
Can you give me your email?

online dating

Sono una ragazza / un ragazzo...
I'm a girl / guy…

tra i xx e xx anni…
between xx and xx years old…

Mi piace un sacco chattare!
I love to chat!

Mandami una e-mail all'indirizzo…
Email me at…

in cerca di un ragazzo / una ragazza…
looking for a guy / a girl…

a cui piace…
who likes…

- talk about your friends
- learn to keep a secret
- insult an enemy
- talk about your family

10. FRIENDS
and FAMILY

best of friends

Ha un cuore grande!
You've got a big heart!
This person will do anything for a friend.

È un tesoro.
He/She's a sweetheart. (Literally: He/She's a treasure.)
Your friend's got a heart of gold, huh?!

È proprio una brava persona.
He/She's a really sweet person.
Too bad there aren't more people like this in the world!

È veramente forte.
He/She's really solid. (Literally: He/She's really strong.)
You can always count on this person in a pinch.

È mitico / un mito!
He/She's a legend! (Literally: He/She's a myth!)
Everyone knows how cool this person is!

È troppo avanti.
He/She's such a trendsetter. (Literally: He/She's too advanced.)
Make sure you follow this person's lead…

È troppo figo/a.
He/She's so cool.
Hope you know a lot of people like this!

ex-friends

È proprio un bel tipo!
He/She's really something!
Meant sarcastically, of course.

Non lo sopporto quel figlio di papà!
I can't stand that momma's boy! (Literally: I can't stand that daddy's son!)
You'll notice the extra accusative "lo" in there—it's not grammatically correct, but everyone says it!

Anna non mi sta per niente simpatica.
I don't like Anna at all.

Non la posso vedere / soffrire / digerire!
I can't stand her! (Literally: I can't see / stand / digest her!)

Mi sta sulle scatole!
He/She ticks me off! (Literally: He/She is on my boxes!)

 Mi sta sulle balle!
He/She pisses me off! (Literally: He/She is on my balls!)
You're really annoyed, huh?!

 Mi sta troppo sul cazzo / sui coglioni!
He/She is a dick! (Literally: He/She is on my dick / balls!)
You've totally had it with this person!

È un povero sfigato.
He's a sore loser.

Mi urta i nervi.
He/She gets on my nerves.
You've had enough of this person, huh?!

gossip

Ho una news fenomenale!
I've got incredible news!

Ho una notizia bomba!
I have a real bomb!

Sai cos'è successo…?
You know what happened…?

Senti questa…
Listen to this…

Non ci crederai, ma…
You won't believe it, but…

La sai l'ultima?!
Heard the latest?

can you keep a secret?

Lo sai mantenere un segreto?
Can you keep a secret?

Acqua in bocca.
Keep it quiet. (Literally: Water in mouth.)

Che rimanga tra noi…
Keep it between the two of us…

Che rimanga tra queste quattro mura…
Keep it within these walls…

Muto come un pesce!
Quiet as a mouse! (Literally: As silent as a fish!)

Portatelo nella tomba.
Take it to the tomb.

spreading rumors

Annalisa è...	Annalisa is...
una che non vale niente.	worthless.
una gran sfigata.	a big loser.
una gran pettegola.	a big gossip.
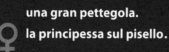 **la principessa sul pisello.**	a princess. (Literally: the princess on the pea)
uno scaricatore di porto.	totally vulgar. (Literally: a docker)

say it as it is

È...	She is...
maliziosa.	bitchy.
cattiva.	mean.
dispettosa.	spiteful.
perfida.	evil.
Ivano è...	Ivano is...
un gran imbecille.	a big imbecile.
un chiacchierone.	a gossip.
un fannullone.	a lazy bum.
uno stupido.	a stupid guy.
un idiota / cazzaro.	an idiot.
un cazzone.	a dick.

YOU'VE JUST BEEN INSULTED? HERE ARE THE BEST WAYS TO REACT

Sei una testa di cazzo!
You dickhead!

Tua madre!
Your mother!

Figlio di buona donna!
Son of a bitch! (Literally: Son of a good woman!)

Figlio di puttana!
Son of a bitch!

Non me ne frega un cazzo / una sega!
I don't give a fuck! (Literally: I don't give a dick / masturbation!)

temper, temper

Non la reggo / sopporto!
I can't stand / take her!

La ucciderei!
I would kill her!

Mi fa una rabbia…
It pissed me off so much…

Sto per scoppiare dalla rabbia!
I'm ready to explode (with anger)!

Ho un incazzo addosso che l'ammazzerei!
I'm so angry that I could kill her/him!

FOR WHEN YOU'VE REALLY HAD ENOUGH

Taci!
Shut up!

Ma stà zitto/a che è meglio!
Shut up, it's better for you!

Non prendermi in giro!
Don't tease me!

Non prendermi per il culo!
Don't fuck with me!
(Literally: Don't take me from my ass!)

Smettila di dire…

cavolate.

baggianate.   Stop bullshitting.

cazzate.

stronzate.

Vai all'inferno!
Go to hell!

Vai a quel paese!
Go to hell! (Literally: Go to that village!)

Vai a cagare!
Go take a shit!

Vai a farti fottere!
Fuck you!

Vaffanculo!
Fuck off!

Sparisci!
Disappear!

cool down

Stai calmo!
Keep calm!

Calmati! Non vale la pena!
Calm down! It isn't worth the worry!

Non farci caso.
Don't worry about it.

Lascialo perdere.
Don't pay attention to him. (Literally: Leave him alone.)

Non dargli retta!
Don't listen to him!

Non badarci! / Fregatene!
Screw it!

family ties

Ci tengo molto...	I care a lot about…
i miei.	my parents.
i miei vecchi.	my old folks.
la mia vecchia.	my old lady.
la mia mammina.	my little mom.
la mia mammona.	my big mom.
la mia mami.	my mom.
il mio vecchio.	my old man.
il mio papi.	my pop.
il mio babbo.	my daddy.
il mio papà.	my dad.

11. FOOD

hungry?

Antonio piace molto...
magnare. ROME
pappare.
sbocconcellare. (Literally: nibbling)
ingozzarsi. (Literally: stuffing himself)

Antonio loves eating.

* In Rome, "Magnare", from "mangiare", means eating;
elsewhere it means eating a lot.

Ho una fame da lupi.
I'm as hungry as a wolf.

Se non mangio, svengo!
If I don't eat, I'll faint!

Ho una fame che mangerei un bue.
I'm so hungry that I could eat an ox.

Cosa non darei per un gelato.
I would give anything for an ice cream.

Sto morendo di sete.
I'm dying of thirst.

Sono disidratato.
I'm dehydrated.

FAST FOOD..

Italians know how to eat well. Fast food joints offer goodies such as: pizza, piadina, gnocchi, tigella (rice croquettes) and other kinds of "stuzzicherie" (snacks). Even though you can eat pretty well, and cheaply, at an Italian fast food stand, going out for a sit-down meal at a nice restaurant is a very popular way to pass a few hours, and there's often live music to enjoy, along with great wine and cocktails.

how was your meal?

Mmh! Che buono!
Mmm! Really good!

È delizioso / squisito!
It's delicious!

È buonissimo!
It's so good!

È una prelibatezza!
It's deliciousness!

HOT! **Che schifo!**
It's gross!

Ha un saporaccio.
It tastes disgusting.

EXTRA HOT! **Fa vomitare!**
It's nasty! (Literally: It makes you vomit!)

HOT! **Che merda!**
What shit!

ITALIAN BARS..

At many Italian bars, you can have just about anything: breakfast, lunch, dinner, snacks, alcoholic and non-alcoholic drinks. Most Italians go to a bar to have a quick cup of good coffee; they often just stand at the bar and drink it down in a few sips—no need to sit at a table! Bars are the coolest spot to have a cocktail and meet friends before going out on the town. Next time you're in an Italian bar, try one of the local's favorite aperitifs: "mojito" (white rum, club soda, brown sugar, and mint leaves), "Negroni®" (gin, red vermouth, bitter Campari®), "caipiroska" (vodka, lime, sugar).

bad manners

Madonna, che mangiata!
God, what a good, hearty meal!

Madonna, che abbuffata!
God, what a feast!

Ho mangiato come un bue.
I ate like a pig. (Literally: I ate like an ox.)

Michele mangia come un maiale.
Michele eats like a pig.

È una fogna.
He/She's a pig. (Literally: He/She's a sewer.)

È un ingordo.
He's a glutton.

Ho mangiato da fare schifo!
It's gross how much I ate!

Sono pieno come un uovo.
I'm full. (Literally: I'm full like an egg.)

eating disorders

Mi viene da...   I feel like...
rimettere.   throwing up.
vomitare.   vomiting.
dare di stomaco.   puking.

Anna mangia come un uccellino / passerotto.
Anna eats like a bird / young sparrow.

12. PARTYING

let's party

Andiamo a…?	Shall we (go)…?
prendere l'aperitivo	have an aperitif
ballare	dance
bere qualcosa	drink something
Conosci…?	Do you know…?
un bar carino	a nice bar
un posticino carino da consigliarmia	a nice place that's recommended?
un bel disco pub	a good club
un bel baretto	a cute little bar
qualche locale X	a hot spot (Literally: some X place)

FANCY GOING OUT TONIGHT?

– **Ti va di uscire stasera?**
Do you want to go out tonight?
– **Mh, dove mi porti? Hai qualche dritta per un localino carino?** Hm, where will you take me?
Can you recommend a nice place?
– **Certo!** Sure!

PARTYING YOUNG…

Italians start partying when they're pretty young. They hang out at local hot spots in town when they're 12 or 13 years old. At around 16, they pass the time away in dance clubs and pizzerias. Many of these clubs and pizzerias serve alcohol and, though the drinking age is officially 18, few places respect the rule.

smoke?

Hai…?

una sigaretta

una siga

una paglia (Literally: a straw)

da fumare (Literally: a smoke)

Do you have a cigarette?

Ti dà fastidio se fumo?
Do you mind if I smoke?

Te ne stai accendendo una dopo l'altra!
You're a chain smoker! (Literally: You're lighting one after the other!)

Mi fai dare due tiri?
Can I have a drag?

Smettila di fumare!
Stop smoking!

THE SMOKING BAN
Since 2005, smoking has been banned in Italy in public buildings, including bars, cafés, restaurants, and offices. According to the law, smoking is allowed only in specially constructed, enclosed smoking areas. Enforcing the law, however, is a different matter. Though fines are heavy, many smokers are fuming over the law, and continue to defy it by lighting up anyway!

drinks

Stasera ho voglia di...	Tonight I want to…
trincare.	drink. *"Trincare" is a popular expression taken from German "trinken".*
bere.	drink.
inciuccarmi.	get drunk.
sballarmi.	get drunk / high.
andare fuori.	get drunk. *(Literally: go out [of one's mind])*
alcolizzarmi.	get drunk.
Andiamo a...?	Should we go…?
farci l'ammazzacaffè	have a stiff drink *(Literally: take a coffee killer)*
farci un bicchiere	have a glass
bere un goccio	drink a drop
farci una birra	for a beer
scolarci una boccia di vino	down a bottle of wine *"Scolarci", comes from the verb "scolarsi" to drain.*
a farci un cicchettino / bicchierino	have a shot

cheers!

Cin cin!
Cheers!

Salute!
To your health!

Alla nostra / tua / vostra!
To our / your health!
"Tua" is singular; "vostra" is plural.

Alla goccia!
To the drop!
Oops, had one too many?

SUFFER THE CONSEQUENCES...

– **Guarda un po'! Elena è già fuori!**
Look! Elena is already drunk!
– **Come? Di già?** What? Already?

WINE, BEER OR PROSECCO?

Wine is the drink of choice for young Italians. It is somewhat of a national drink and Italy produces many varieties. Prices are reasonable too. Beer—Italian or otherwise—is popular with 20-somethings. Hipsters like to start off the evening sipping aperitifs, then spend the rest of the evening at a pizzeria, lounging over good food and great wine. Popular drinks in clubs include high-proof spirits mixed with fruit juice. Those with money to burn reserve a table at trendy clubs in order to "be seen" with their drink of choice — usually Prosecco.

under the influence

Maria beve come una spugna.
Maria is a heavy drinker. (Literally: Maria drinks like a sponge.)

Ho bevuto un casino.
I drank a lot.
"Casino" is a word that means many things: brothel, mess—but as an adverb, like in this case, it means a lot.

Ho bevuto da fare schifo!
I drank so much, it's gross!

Guarda che si sta inciuccando!
Look how he/she is getting drunk!

the high life

Si è fatto/a...	
una canna. (Literally: a cane)	He/She smoked
una tromba. (Literally: a trumpet)	a joint.
uno spino. (Literally: a thorn)	
un joint.	

È...	He/She's...
fumato/a.	high. (Literally: smoked)
incannato/a duro.	high. (Literally: under the effect of canes)
fatto/a duro.	into drugs. (Literally: hard done)
sotto acido.	on acid.
fuori.	out.
andato/a.	gone.

Che viaggio! / È un gran viaggio!
What a trip!

Non prendo droghe.
I don't do drugs.

the morning after

Francesco…

è ubriaco duro / fradicio.
  (Literally: is a hard / soaked drunk)

è bresco. BOLOGNA
si è preso una gran ciucca.
  (Literally: took a great drink)

Francesco is drunk.

è fuori come un balcone.
  (Literally: is out like a balcony)

HOT! **è fuori come un culo.**
  (Literally: is out like an ass)

è ciucco.

STREET FIGHTERS

Ieri sera hanno fatto a botte.
Last night they had a fight.

È scattata la rissa.
There was a fight.

Hanno fatto a botte / a pugni!
They threw punches!

Mario le ha prese.
Mario was beaten up.

Lo hanno preso a cazzotti.
They punched him.

busted!

Attento! C'è la pula!
Watch out! The cops!

Occhio ai pullotti!
Watch out for cops! (Literally: Eye the cops!)

Attento, questa strada è piena di autovelox!
Watch out! There are tons of speed cameras on this road!

Occhio, qua multano di brutto!
Watch out! They give out lots of fines here!

TELLING THE STORY...

Mi sono beccato una multa per...	I got a ticket for...
eccesso di velocità.	speeding.
esser passato con il rosso.	going through a red light.
non aver rispettato lo stop.	rolling through a stop.
non aver dato la precedenza.	not giving way.

YIKES! LOCKED UP AND STAYING THERE...

Lo hanno messo...	He got arrested.
dentro.	(Literally: inside)
in gabbia.	(Literally: into the cage)
al fresco.	(Literally: at the fresh)
in gattabuia.	(Literally: into prison)

music

Mi piace…	I love…
la musica pop.	pop music.
il rock italiano.	Italian rock.
la musica rock.	rock music.
la musica anni '80/'90.	the music of the 80s/90s.
la salsa e merengue.	salsa & merengue.
la latino-americana.	Latin-American music.
il liscio.	ballroom music.
la techno.	techno.
la musica classica.	classical music.
l'house.	house.
il raggae.	reggae.
l'hip-hop.	hip-hop.
la ska.	ska.

Impazzisco per il rock.
I'm crazy about rock.

Sono un fanatico della musica classica.
I'm a classical music fanatic.

L'house mi piace un casino.
I really love house music.

live music

Sono stato ad un concerto…	I went to a…concert.
favoloso.	fabulous
spettacolare.	spectacular
meraviglioso.	great
troppo figo.	cool (Literally: too cool)
della Madonna.	great
da paura.	great (Literally: fearful)
schifoso.	awful
deludente.	disappointing
di merda.	shitty

(HOT!)

Mi piace ascoltare la musica a palla / a manetta.
NORTHERN ITALY
I like to hear music at full blast. (Literally: I like to hear music at
ball / at handcuff.)

ALL KINDS OF MUSIC…
Italians listen to all kinds of music, including local
and international favorites. Funny thing is, the Italian
singers who are popular abroad—Eros Ramazzotti,
Nek, Laura Pausini—are not so popular in Italy.
Youth prefer rock. Italian bands such as Vasco Rossi,
Ligabue, Piero Pelù are adored in Italy and not so well
known internationally.

tune in to tv

Mi piace un sacco...	I really like...
i cartoni animati.	cartoons.
le soap.	soaps.
il tg.	the news.
i reality show.	reality shows.
i quiz televisivi.	game shows.

Dove hai messo la guida TV?
Where did you put the TV listing?

Mi passi il telecomando?
Can you give me the remote?

Non cambiare!
Don't change (the channel)!

Ti va di andare al cinema?
What about a movie?

Ci prendiamo un DVD?
Should we rent a DVD?

movie fan?

Vorrei vedere…	I'd like to see a/an…
un film d'azione.	action movie.
un film d'amore.	romance movie.
un film dell'orrore.	horror movie.
un giallo / noir.	thriller.
L'avete…	Do you have it…
in italiano?	in Italian?
in lingua originale?	in the original language?
sottotitolato?	with subtitles?

REALITY SHOWS…

Although Italians love to be out socializing, they can spend entire days watching reality shows. Italians, much like people elsewhere, have a love-hate relationship with them. In fact, many Italians use the English word "trash" to refer to reality shows—so if you hear this word, you know what they are talking about.

ITALIANS ARE FAMOUS ALL AROUND THE WORLD FOR THEIR NON-VERBAL LANGUAGE - NOBODY CAN GESTURE LIKE AN ITALIAN!

COSA DICI? / MA CHE CAZZO VUOI?

What the hell do you want?

Use this typical Italian gesture to express your annoyance.

MA SEI FUORI?

Are you crazy?

(Literally: Are you out [of your mind]?)

VAFFANCULO!

Fuck off!

The gesture says it all…

TI FACCIO UN CULO COSI!
I'll make you such an ass!
This threatening gesture is used to show that someone is going to get a beating—physically or mentally.

DIMENTICAVO!
I forgot!
Duh!

AL BACIO!
Great! (Literally: Like a kiss!)
Use this gesture to show that something— or someone—is fantastic.

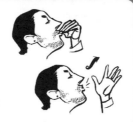

CHE BUONO!
Yummy!
Delicious, right?!

I UN RICCHIONE!
He's gay!
(Literally: He's a big ear!)
*This is downright nasty
and rude—be careful!*

HO TROMBATO!
I had sex!
*The verb "trombare" is
a slang variation of the
word "tromba" trumpet.*

UNA SEGA!
Masturbating!
*You know this is a dirty
one…!*